BESLEY'S BRITAIN

Your Good Holiday Guide

SOUVENIR PRESS

First published 1984 by Souvenir Press Ltd,
43 Great Russell Street, London WC1B 3PA
and simultaneously in Canada

ISBN 0 285 62645 0

Printed in Great Britain by
Ebenezer Baylis & Son Limited,
The Trinity Press, Worcester, and London

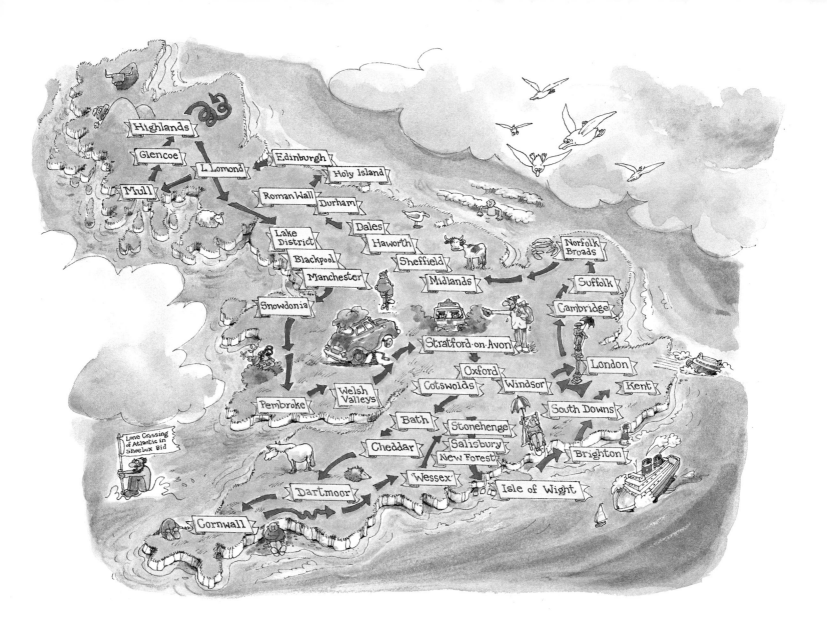

A friendly welcome to start the journey...

Home Counties: settling down to a quiet pub lunch.

Tranquil moments in Royal Windsor.

Controlling the queue to the Tower of London.

London Traffic: hazards of crossing the Mall.

Palace of Westminster: the Nation thrills to the cut and thrust of Parliamentary debate.

Piccadilly Circus: pulsating centre of amusement and revels...

The Romance of Punting along the Cambridge Backs...

Historic Lavenham: traditional plumbing in rural Suffolk . . .

Getting away from it all on the Norfolk Broads.

Taking advantage of the weather to visit a Stately Home . . .

Exploring Sheffield's industrial past...

Brontë Country: Soaking in the atmosphere of Haworth Parsonage.

Sheepdog training in the Yorkshire Dales.

Hadrian's Wall: scene of savage encounters ...

Durham Cathedral: final resting-place of Cuthbert's bones.

Holy Island: Sunbathing on the beach at Lindisfarne.

Joining in the fun of the Edinburgh Festival.

Pausing to enjoy the views along Loch Lomond.

Loitering within tent on the Island of Mull

Nightfall in Glencoe.

Traffic delays in the Highlands of Scotland.

Lake District: the Keep-Fit Craze Sweeps Cumbria...

Blackpool Illuminations: following the traffic lights along the Golden Mile...

Greater Manchester: the fun of shopping in faraway places...

Snowdonia: towering peaks and scenic grandeur...

Bird-spotting on the Pembroke Coast.

Welsh National Costume: the search continues...

Checking into the hotel at Stratford-upon-Avon: to sleep perchance ...

Leisurely scenes on the Inland Waterways.

Peace and Quiet in the Cotswolds.

Oxford: trying to find the University.

Getting immersed in the culture of Bath...

Cheddar Gorge: a spectacular cleft created by the constant stream of coaches.

Dartmoor – haunt of the fearsome Hound of the Baskervilles...

Probing the Cornish coast in search of surprises...

Pastoral scenes in Hardy's Wessex...

Breakfast at Stonehenge

Salisbury Cathedral: photographing England's tallest spire.

Village cricket: tension and drama in the New Forest.

Cowes, Isle of Wight...   when it's not Cowes Week.

South Coast: looking for somewhere to retire for the night.

Getting changed on the famous beach at Brighton.

Dining out in the South Downs: a final celebration.

Boosting British industry: gifts for the folks back home.